W9-BTR-296

contents

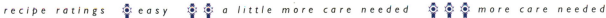

recipe ratings   ❋ *easy*   ❋❋ *a little more care needed*   ❋❋❋ *more care needed*

Tortellini with creamy mushroom sauce

Fresh tortellini, small pasta parcels containing meat, cheese or vegetable fillings, are now available in Italian markets and supermarkets, making this delicious dish very easy to put together.

Preparation time **15 minutes**
Total cooking time **35 minutes**
Serves 4

3 tablespoons unsalted butter
2 shallots, finely chopped
I lb. button mushrooms, thinly sliced
I tablespoon lemon juice
2 tablespoons port
2 cups heavy cream
I lb. fresh tortellini

1 Over low heat, melt the butter in a skillet and cook the shallots with a pinch of salt for 3–5 minutes without coloring. Toss the mushrooms in the lemon juice, add to the pan with another pinch of salt and cook over medium heat for about 10–15 minutes, or until the mushrooms are dry and all the liquid has evaporated. Add the port and cook for 2–3 minutes, or until almost dry, being careful to not let the mixture scorch. Stir in the cream and simmer for about 5–10 minutes, or until the sauce is thick enough to coat the back of a spoon. Check for seasoning.

2 Meanwhile, bring a large saucepan of salted water to a boil. Add a splash of oil to stop the pasta from sticking and cook the tortellini according to the manufacturer's instructions. Drain well and divide the tortellini among four warm plates. Spoon the sauce over and serve with freshly ground black pepper.

Chef's tip For a stronger flavor, mix some soaked dried mushrooms, such as porcini (cèpes) or shiitake, with the button mushrooms.

Linguine vongole

Linguine, the Italian word for "little tongues," are long flat noodles. Here they are teamed with fresh clams in a creamy white wine and parsley sauce. A little time-consuming to make, but well worth the effort.

Preparation time **25 minutes + 1 hour soaking**
Total cooking time **50 minutes**
Serves 4–6

4 lb. fresh littleneck or cherrystone clams
1/3 cup plus 1 tablespoon unsalted butter
1 large onion, finely chopped
1 large stalk celery, thinly sliced
2 sprigs of fresh thyme
1 bay leaf
8 stems of fresh parsley
8 cloves garlic, chopped
1 cup sliced button mushrooms
3 cups dry white wine
1 lb. dried linguine
3 tablespoons all-purpose flour
1 1/2 cups heavy cream
1/3 cup chopped fresh flat-leaf parsley

1 Wash the clams, then soak for 1 hour in cold water, changing the water several times. While the clams are soaking, melt the 1/3 cup butter in a large stockpot. Add the onion and cook over low heat for 5 minutes, then add the celery, thyme, bay leaf, parsley stems, garlic, mushrooms and wine. Bring to a boil and cook for

5 minutes. Add the drained clams and cook, covered, for 5–8 minutes (15–20 minutes for large clams), or until they open. Remove the clams with a slotted spoon, discarding any that are unopened, and set aside to cool. Remove the meat from half the clam shells, rinse under cold water, drain and coarsely chop. Boil the sauce for another 10 minutes, then strain through a strainer lined with damp cheesecloth. Measure out 1 1/2 cups of the cooking liquid.

2 Bring a large saucepan of salted water to a boil. Add a splash of oil to stop the pasta from sticking and cook the linguine according to the manufacturer's instructions. Drain well, toss with a little olive oil and keep warm.

3 Over low heat, melt the 1 tablespoon of butter in a saucepan. Stir in the flour and cook for 2 minutes. Remove from the heat and gradually whisk in the reserved cooking liquid. Return to the heat and bring to a boil, stirring constantly. Reduce the heat to low and simmer for 5 minutes, or until thickened. Whisk in the cream and simmer for another 5 minutes. Add the whole and chopped clams, parsley and some salt and freshly ground black pepper. Cook for 30 seconds and serve over the linguine.

Chef's tip Small clams are less tough than large clams.

Spinach pasta salad

Combining Roquefort, bacon and walnuts with the bright green tagliatelle creates a winning formula.

Preparation time **20 minutes**
Total cooking time **10 minutes**
Serves 4

PASTA
1²/3 cups all-purpose flour
1/2 teaspoon salt
4 teaspoons olive oil
2 eggs, lightly beaten
3 tablespoons frozen spinach, thawed, squeezed dry and
  very finely chopped

1 shallot, finely chopped
1 clove garlic, finely chopped
3 tablespoons white wine vinegar
1/2 cup walnut oil
3 oz. Roquefort cheese, cut into cubes
1 small red onion, thinly sliced
4 slices bacon, crisply fried and coarsely crumbled
1/2 cup walnuts, browned in the bacon drippings
1 tablespoon chopped fresh parsley

1 To make the pasta, follow the method in the Chef's techniques on page 62, adding the spinach with the eggs. Divide the dough in half and pass through the pasta machine. When the pasta sheets have passed through the thinnest setting, pass through the 1/4-inch cutters to make tagliatelle (see Chef's techniques, page 63).
2 To make the vinaigrette, combine the shallot, garlic, vinegar, oil, salt and pepper and whisk until blended.
3 Bring a large saucepan of salted water to a boil. Add a splash of oil to stop the pasta from sticking and cook the tagliatelle for 2–3 minutes, or until *al dente*. Drain, run under cold water, then drain once more.
4 Combine the pasta and vinaigrette in a bowl. Add the remaining ingredients and toss well to combine.

Cannelloni

These pasta tubes are stuffed with a succulent meat filling, coated with a creamy cheese sauce and baked in the oven until piping hot and golden brown. Perfect for lunch served with a crisp green salad.

*Preparation time **50 minutes***
*Total cooking time **55 minutes***

Serves 4

¹/₃ cup fresh bread crumbs
1 tablespoon milk
4 teaspoons unsalted butter
1 onion, finely chopped
3 oz. pork tenderloin or lean pork from the shoulder
5 oz. skinless, boneless chicken breast halves
¹/₃ cup whipping cream
¹/₄ cup chopped fresh parsley
¹/₃ cup freshly grated Parmesan
1 egg white, lightly beaten
1 oz. prosciutto, diced
12 dried cannelloni or manicotti tubes (see Chef's tips)

SAUCE
¹/₄ cup unsalted butter
¹/₃ cup all-purpose flour
2 cups milk
¹/₂ cup shredded Gruyère cheese

1 Preheat the oven to 350°F. Soak the bread crumbs in the milk. Heat the butter in a small skillet, add the onion and cook gently until soft and translucent. In a meat grinder or food processor, grind the pork and chicken and transfer to a bowl. Add the soaked bread crumbs, cream, parsley, Parmesan and enough egg white to hold the filling together. Add the prosciutto and cooked onion. Season well.

2 Spoon the meat mixture into a pastry bag fitted with a large nozzle. Fill each cannelloni tube with the filling.

3 To make the sauce, melt 3 tablespoons of the butter in a saucepan over medium heat. Add the flour and whisk for 3 minutes. Remove from the heat and gradually add the milk. Return to the heat and whisk until the mixture boils and is thick enough to coat the back of a spoon. Whisk in the cheese until melted, then stir in the remaining butter. Spread a thin layer of sauce over the bottom of an 11 x 7 x 2-inch (or 8 x 8-inch) baking dish and place the filled cannelloni tubes on top. Pour the remaining sauce over and bake for 25 minutes covered, then bake for about 15–20 minutes uncovered, or until lightly colored.

Chef's tips Instead of grinding the meat yourself, you could use ready-made ground lean pork and chicken.

If you can't find cannelloni tubes, you can replace them by lightly cooking 12 lasagna sheets and then carefully rolling them up into tube shapes.

Italian meatballs

Tasty meatballs cooked in a rich tomato sauce and served with spaghetti make a warming winter dish.
The meatballs may be made from ground beef or a combination of ground pork and veal if preferred.

*Preparation time **50 minutes***
*Total cooking time **1 hour 25 minutes***
Serves 4

¹/3 cup olive oil
1 onion, finely chopped
2 cloves garlic, finely chopped
¹/4 teaspoon chopped fresh oregano
1 lb. lean ground beef
1 egg, lightly beaten
1 lb. dried spaghetti
freshly grated Parmesan, to serve

SAUCE
3 tablespoons olive oil
1 large onion, finely chopped
3 x 16 oz. cans whole peeled plum tomatoes,
  undrained and puréed in a food mill or food
  processor
5 cloves garlic, finely chopped
1 bay leaf
2 sprigs of fresh thyme

1 Heat half the oil in a small skillet over gentle heat and cook the onion for 5–7 minutes, or until soft. Off the heat, add the garlic and oregano and stir well. Strain off any excess oil and set aside to cool. Once cooled, add to the meat and mix well. Season with salt and pepper and add enough of the egg to bind the mixture together.
2 Divide the meat into eight portions and roll into smooth balls. Heat the remaining olive oil in a large skillet and cook the meatballs until browned all over. Transfer to a plate lined with paper towels to drain.
3 To make the sauce, heat the olive oil in a saucepan and slowly cook the onion for 5 minutes, without coloring. Add the tomatoes, garlic, bay leaf, thyme and the meatballs and simmer over low heat, covered, for 20 minutes. Remove the cover and simmer for another 30–40 minutes, skimming as needed. Remove the bay leaf and thyme and season to taste with salt and pepper.
4 Bring a large saucepan of salted water to a boil. Add a splash of oil to stop the pasta from sticking and cook the pasta according to the manufacturer's instructions.
5 Drain well and transfer the pasta to a large platter or individual plates. Top with the sauce and meatballs. Serve with the Parmesan on the side.

Spaghetti bolognese

Spaghetti bolognese, which reflects the rich style of the cooking of Bologna, in northern Italy, is undoubtedly one of the best-known and most well-loved Italian pasta dishes.

*Preparation time **50 minutes***
*Total cooking time **1 hour 10 minutes***
Serves 6–8

1/2 **cup olive oil**
2 lb. lean ground beef
I large onion, finely chopped
3 tablespoons tomato paste
1/3 **cup red wine**
8 cloves garlic, finely chopped
5 lb. fresh tomatoes, peeled, seeded and puréed in a
 food mill or food processor
4 sprigs of fresh thyme
I bay leaf
I 1/2 **lb. dried spaghetti**
freshly grated Parmesan, to serve

1 In a large saucepan, heat half the oil until very hot. Add the beef, season with salt and pepper, and brown for 10 minutes, or until the liquid from the meat has evaporated. Strain off the fat and set the meat aside. Heat the remaining oil, add the onion and cook for 5 minutes, without coloring. Add the tomato paste and cook for 1–2 minutes, then add the wine and cook for 5 minutes. Transfer the meat back to the pan, add the garlic, tomatoes, thyme and bay leaf and simmer for 45 minutes, or until the liquid has reduced by half. Remove the thyme and bay leaf.

2 Meanwhile, bring a large saucepan of salted water to a boil. Add a splash of oil to stop the pasta from sticking and cook the spaghetti according to the manufacturer's instructions. Drain well and transfer to individual plates. Pour the sauce over and serve with the Parmesan.

Fettuccine Alfredo

A delicious creamy dish that is simple and quick to make. For good results, however, it is essential to use freshly grated Parmesan, as store-bought grated Parmesan is usually a poor substitute.

*Preparation time **5 minutes***
*Total cooking time **15 minutes***
Serves 4

I 1/2 **cups heavy cream**
2 1/4 **cups freshly grated Parmesan**
1/4 **cup chopped fresh flat-leaf parsley**
I lb. dried fettuccine
freshly grated Parmesan, to serve

1 Place the cream in a heavy-bottomed saucepan and bring to a boil. Gradually whisk in the Parmesan. Add the parsley, salt and freshly ground black pepper and stir until well combined.

2 Meanwhile, bring a large saucepan of salted water to a boil. Add a splash of oil to stop the pasta from sticking and cook the fettuccine according to the manufacturer's instructions. Drain well and toss with the cream sauce. Serve with freshly grated Parmesan on the side.

Chèvre cheese ravioli with fennel purée

A little effort and patience is required to produce this outstanding dish, which will impress friends and family alike. The fresh tomato sauce and delicate flavor of the fennel combine superbly with the ravioli.

Preparation time **1 hour + 15 minutes freezing**
Total cooking time **1 hour**
Serves **4**

PASTA
3/4 cup all-purpose flour
pinch of salt
2 teaspoons olive oil
I egg, lightly beaten

6 oz. chèvre cheese, cut into 18–20 slices
I egg, lightly beaten

FENNEL PUREE
I medium fennel bulb, sliced
I shallot, sliced
I cup chicken stock
sprig of fresh thyme
I bay leaf

TOMATO SAUCE
I shallot, finely chopped
2 cloves garlic, finely chopped
4 tomatoes, peeled, seeded and quartered
sprig of fresh thyme
pinch of sugar

BUTTER SAUCE
2 teaspoons unsalted butter
I shallot, chopped
1/3 cup white wine
sprig of fresh thyme
1/2 bay leaf
1/4 cup whipping cream
1/2 cup unsalted butter, chilled and cut into cubes
I teaspoon lemon juice

1 To make the pasta, follow the method in the Chef's techniques on page 62, dividing the dough into two pieces before passing through the pasta machine. Pass the pieces through the thinnest setting on the machine, making sure they are at least 61/2 inches wide.

2 Place the goats' cheese on one sheet of pasta, so that the slices are about 11/2 inches apart and 11/2 inches from the edges. Brush the pasta around the cheese with the egg. Place the second sheet on top and press firmly around each mound to expel any air and to seal. Cut out the ravioli by pressing a 21/2–3-inch biscuit cutter down firmly, or by using a rolling cutter to make 21/2–3-inch squares. Place in a single layer between sheets of waxed paper and freeze for 15 minutes (see Chef's techniques, page 63).

3 To make the fennel purée, cook the fennel gently with the shallot in a few tablespoons of the stock, covered, for 10 minutes. Add the herbs and remaining stock, cover and simmer for 15 minutes, or until tender. Drain off the excess liquid, discard the herbs and purée the fennel and shallot in a food processor.

4 To make the tomato sauce, heat some oil in a pan, add all the ingredients and season. Cook gently, stirring occasionally, for 10 minutes, or until the sauce is thick.

5 To make the butter sauce, heat the butter in a pan, add the shallot and cook for 3 minutes. Add the wine and herbs and simmer for 5 minutes, or until the liquid has reduced by half. Add the cream, heat to gently simmering, then reduce the heat to low. Gradually whisk in the butter, without allowing the sauce to boil. Stir in the lemon juice, strain, cover and keep warm.

6 Bring a large saucepan of salted water to a boil. Add a splash of oil to stop the pasta from sticking and cook the ravioli for 3–4 minutes, or until *al dente*. Drain well. To serve, spoon the fennel purée into the center of four plates. Place some ravioli on top, coat with the butter sauce and spread a little tomato sauce around the edge.

Pasta marinara

*Using canned tomatoes will always give a deep red sauce and allows this dish
to be made, and therefore enjoyed, all year round.*

Preparation time **20 minutes**
Total cooking time **1 hour 15 minutes**
Serves 4–6

¹/₂ cup loosely packed fresh basil leaves
2 sprigs of fresh thyme
1 bay leaf
3 tablespoons olive oil
1 large onion, finely chopped
4 x 16 oz. cans whole peeled plum tomatoes,
  undrained and puréed in a food mill or food
  processor
5 cloves garlic, finely chopped
1 lb. dried rigatoni or penne rigate
freshly grated Parmesan, to serve

1 Separate the basil leaves, keeping the stems for the
sauce. Tie the stems in a bundle with the sprigs of thyme
and bay leaf.

2 In a large saucepan, heat the olive oil and slowly cook
the onion for 5 minutes without coloring. Add the
tomatoes, garlic and herb bundle. Bring to a boil, reduce
the heat to low and simmer, covered, for 40 minutes,
then uncovered for another 20 minutes, stirring from
time to time. Season to taste with salt and pepper.

3 Bring a large saucepan of salted water to a boil. Add
a splash of oil to stop the pasta from sticking and cook
the rigatoni or penne according to the manufacturer's
instructions. Drain well, toss with a little olive oil and
keep warm.

4 When the sauce is ready, remove the bundle of herbs
and discard. Finely chop the basil leaves and mix in with
the sauce. Do not let it boil again.

5 Toss the sauce with the cooked pasta and serve with
the Parmesan.

Chef's tip This sauce can be made with fresh tomatoes,
but this is recommended only if the tomatoes are in
season. Do not use winter tomatoes because they are
mainly water with very little flavor and color. If good
tomatoes are available, use the same quantity as in the
recipe, peeling and removing the seeds. Depending on
the ripeness of the tomatoes, it may be necessary to add
1 tablespoon tomato paste to reinforce the color and
flavor. After the onions have cooked, add the tomato
paste and cook for 1–2 minutes before adding the
remaining ingredients.

Pasta with seafood sauce

For this recipe, you can use any variety of seafood, but do not overcook it or it can become tough.

Preparation time **20 minutes**
Total cooking time **1 hour 40 minutes**
Serves 4–6

2 sprigs of fresh thyme
2 sprigs of fresh parsley
1 bay leaf
1/2 cup olive oil
1 large onion, finely chopped
1/2 cup white wine
3 x 16 oz. cans whole peeled plum tomatoes,
    undrained and puréed in a food processor
5 cloves garlic, finely chopped
8–10 firmly closed small fresh mussels, scrubbed clean
8 oz. fresh or frozen thawed scallops, patted dry
8 oz. cleaned squid (calamari) hoods, sliced into rings
1 lb. cooked medium shrimp, peeled
1/2 cup chopped fresh flat-leaf parsley
1 lb. dried spaghetti

1 Tie the herbs and bay leaf in a bundle. Heat two thirds of the oil in a saucepan and cook the onion for 5 minutes without coloring. Add the wine and simmer until reduced by three-quarters. Add the tomatoes, garlic and herbs and simmer, covered, for 20 minutes, then uncovered for 40 minutes. Add the mussels and simmer for 5 minutes until they open. Discard any unopened ones.
2 Heat the remaining oil in a skillet and fry the scallops and squid for 1 minute, or until firm and white. Add to the sauce with the shrimp and heat through. Remove the herbs and mix in the parsley.
3 Bring a large saucepan of salted water to a boil. Add a splash of oil to stop the pasta from sticking and cook the spaghetti according to the manufacturer's instructions. Season the sauce and pour over the drained pasta.

Classic lasagna

Although you can make this very popular classic Italian dish with store-bought lasagna noodles, the flavor and texture of thinly rolled fresh pasta is quite unique and well worth the effort.

Preparation time 1 hour + 20 minutes resting
Total cooking time 2 hours 15 minutes
Serves 10–12

olive oil, for cooking
2 lb. lean ground beef
I large onion, finely chopped
1/4 cup tomato paste
1/2 cup red wine
8 cloves garlic, finely chopped
4 x 16 oz. cans peeled plum tomatoes, undrained and
    puréed in a food mill or processor
4 sprigs of fresh thyme
I bay leaf
1 1/4 lb. ricotta cheese
1/3 cup heavy cream
4 eggs
12 oz. mozzarella cheese, thinly sliced
1/2 cup freshly grated Parmesan

PASTA
3 1/3 cups all-purpose flour
I teaspoon salt
3 tablespoons olive oil
4 eggs, lightly beaten

1 Heat 2 tablespoons oil in a saucepan, add the beef and brown over high heat for 10 minutes, or until the liquid has almost evaporated. Strain off the fat and set the meat aside. Reduce the heat, add a little more oil and cook the onion for 5 minutes, without coloring. Add the tomato paste and cook for 1–2 minutes, then add the wine, garlic, tomatoes, herbs and beef and simmer for 1 hour, or until the liquid has reduced by half.

2 To make the pasta, follow the method in the Chef's techniques on page 62, dividing the dough into four pieces before passing through the pasta machine to a thickness of 1/16–1/8 inch. Cut into 5 x 4-inch rectangles.

3 Bring a large saucepan of salted water to a boil. Add a splash of oil to stop the pasta sticking and cook the lasagna in batches for 2–3 minutes, or until *al dente*. Transfer to a bowl of cold water, then drain and put between clean towels.

4 Drain the ricotta in a strainer, then mix with the cream and eggs in a bowl. Season, cover and set aside. Preheat the oven to 375°F.

5 Spread 3/4 cup of the meat sauce in a 9 x 13-inch baking dish. Place a layer of pasta on top, then a third of the ricotta mixture, then some sauce. Repeat the layers twice more and finish with pasta covered with sauce. Cover with the cheeses. Bake for 45 minutes, or until golden. Leave for 20 minutes before cutting.

Saffron pasta with oven-dried tomatoes and lima beans

The yellow pasta, deep red tomatoes and green lima beans make this a very colorful, as well as delicious, pasta dish. Either cream cheese or Italian ricotta may be used, and the quantity of stock may be increased to make a more liquid sauce.

Preparation time 1 hour + 15 minutes soaking
Total cooking time 1 hour 40 minutes
Serves 6 as a starter

PASTA
pinch of saffron threads
2¹/2 cups all-purpose flour
1 teaspoon salt
2 teaspoons olive oil
3 eggs, lightly beaten

15 cherry tomatoes
2–3 sprigs of fresh thyme
12 oz. shelled fresh or frozen baby lima beans
¹/3 cup olive oil
2 cloves garlic, crushed
¹/4 cup cream cheese or ricotta
³/4 cup vegetable or light chicken stock
²/3 cup freshly grated Parmesan

1 Preheat the oven to 300°F. Soak the saffron in 1 tablespoon hot water for 15 minutes.
2 To make the pasta, follow the method in the Chef's techniques on page 62, and add the saffron threads and

their liquid with the eggs. Divide the dough into four pieces before passing through the pasta machine. When the pasta has passed through the thinnest setting, pass the sheets through the ¹/4-inch cutters to make tagliatelle (see Chef's techniques, page 63).

3 Halve the tomatoes across their equator and place them on a baking sheet. Sprinkle with the thyme leaves and some salt, and bake for 1¹/4–1¹/2 hours, or until dry but still soft to the touch. Remove and allow to cool.

4 Add the beans to a saucepan of boiling water and cook for about 6 minutes, or until tender. Drain and allow to cool.

5 Bring a large saucepan of salted water to a boil. Add a splash of oil to prevent the pasta from sticking and cook the tagliatelle for 2–3 minutes, or until *al dente*. Drain well.

6 Heat half the oil in a large skillet and fry the garlic to light brown. Place the cream cheese or ricotta and stock in a food processor, add the garlic and process until smooth. Return the mixture to the pan and warm through. Add half the tomatoes, the beans, Parmesan, remaining olive oil and the tagliatelle. Toss together and season to taste with salt and freshly ground black pepper. Serve with the remaining tomatoes scattered over the top.

Winter squash ravioli with basil butter

The unusual and delicate flavor of the squash and herb filling is perfectly complemented by the basil and garlic butter. When making ravioli, it is important to roll the pasta as thinly as possible, making sure that it doesn't tear when handled.

Preparation time **1 hour 30 minutes**
Total cooking time **1 hour 20 minutes**
Serves **6–8**

12 oz. piece butternut or hubbard squash

2 tablespoons olive oil

3 oz. prosciutto, finely chopped

1/2 cup freshly grated Parmesan

3 tablespoons chopped fresh basil

1/4 cup chopped fresh sage

1 egg yolk

2 tablespoons heavy cream

pinch of nutmeg

PASTA

3 1/3 cups all-purpose flour

1 teaspoon salt

3 tablespoons olive oil

4 eggs, lightly beaten

HERB SAUCE

3/4 cup unsalted butter or olive oil

6 cloves garlic, halved

2/3 cup firmly packed fresh basil leaves

1 Preheat the oven to 375°F. Place the squash on a lightly oiled baking sheet and brush with the olive oil. Bake for about 1 hour, or until the flesh is soft when pressed lightly with a spoon. Set aside.

2 To make the pasta, follow the method in the Chef's techniques on page 62, dividing the dough into four

pieces before passing through the pasta machine. Pass the pieces through the thinnest setting on the machine, making sure they are at least 6 1/2 inches wide, then trim horizontally into 5-inch wide strips.

3 Once the squash has cooled, scrape out the flesh and mash in a bowl. Stir in the prosciutto, Parmesan, basil, sage, egg yolk and cream. Season with the nutmeg, salt and pepper. Cover and set aside.

4 Spoon heaped teaspoons of the squash mixture at 2 1/2-inch intervals along the pasta strips. Lightly brush with water around the edges of the squash. Lay another sheet of pasta on top and press firmly around each mound to expel any air and to seal. Cut out the ravioli by pressing a 2 1/2-inch biscuit cutter down firmly, then flour lightly. Place in a single layer between sheets of waxed paper and refrigerate until ready to use (see Chef's techniques, page 63).

5 Bring a large saucepan of salted water to a boil. Add a splash of oil to stop the pasta from sticking and cook the ravioli in batches for 5–6 minutes, or until they float and are *al dente*. Drain well.

6 To make the herb sauce, melt the butter over low heat, then add the garlic and let infuse for a few minutes. The longer you do this, the stronger the garlic flavor, but take care not to allow the garlic to brown. Take the pan off the heat and remove the garlic with a slotted spoon. Tear the basil and add to the sauce.

7 Toss the ravioli with the basil sauce to reheat and coat well. Serve on warm plates.

Chef's tips For an extra garnish, scatter some roasted, lightly salted pepitas around the ravioli.

Pasta with Parmesan and Gruyère

A quick, simple dish that may be made using fresh or dry pasta. It also makes a good accompaniment to broiled meats.

Preparation time **20 minutes**
Total cooking time **25 minutes**
Serves **4**

PASTA
3¹/₃ cups all-purpose flour
1 teaspoon salt
3 tablespoons olive oil
4 eggs, lightly beaten

¹/₄ cup olive oil
¹/₃ cup freshly shredded Gruyère cheese
1 cup freshly grated Parmesan
extra block of Parmesan, to make shavings

1 To make the pasta, follow the method in the Chef's techniques on page 62. Divide the dough into four before passing through the pasta machine. When the pasta has passed through the thinnest setting, pass the sheets through the ¹/₄-inch cutters to make tagliatelle (see Chef's techniques, page 63).
2 Bring a large saucepan of salted water to a boil. Add a splash of oil to stop the pasta from sticking and cook the tagliatelle for 2–3 minutes, or until *al dente*.
3 Drain the pasta well, place in a large bowl and pour in the olive oil. Season and toss with the Gruyère and grated Parmesan. Place in a serving dish and top with Parmesan shavings and freshly ground black pepper.

Chef's tip Parmesan shavings are an easy decoration to make. Take a block of Parmesan and draw a vegetable peeler along one side to make thin shavings.

Spaghetti carbonara

The pasta must be well drained and extremely hot when tossed in the sauce, as it is the heat of the pasta that lightly cooks the egg yolks.

Preparation time **10 minutes**
Total cooking time **20 minutes**
Serves **4–6**

¹/₃ cup oil
8 oz. slab bacon, cut into ¹/₂-inch cubes
1 lb. dried spaghetti
8 egg yolks
1 cup freshly grated Parmesan
3 tablespoons chopped fresh parsley

1 Heat the oil in a skillet and add the bacon. Brown for 5–10 minutes, or until the bacon is crisp and evenly colored. Drain, then place on paper towels. Set aside.
2 Bring a large saucepan of salted water to a boil. Add a splash of oil to stop the pasta from sticking and cook the pasta according to the manufacturer's instructions.
3 Just before the pasta has finished cooking, whisk the egg yolks in a large bowl and season with freshly ground black pepper. Whisk in ¹/₄ cup boiling water and the Parmesan. Drain the spaghetti well and toss the hot pasta with the egg and cheese mixture. Toss in the bacon and serve immediately with a little parsley sprinkled over the top.

Pasta with Parmesan and Gruyère (top)
and Spaghetti carbonara

Ricotta shells

The extensive cooking time for this dish may seem alarming at first glance; however, it is worth noting that, in fact, both the rich tomato sauce and the finished cheese-and-herb stuffed pasta shells spend much time cooking in the oven, leaving you free to do other things.

Preparation time **1 hour**
Total cooking time **2 hours 30 minutes**
Serves **4**

3 tablespoons unsalted butter
2 oz. slab bacon, diced
1 small onion, chopped
1 small carrot, chopped
3 tablespoons tomato paste
1 tablespoon all-purpose flour
1 lb. tomatoes, peeled, seeded and chopped
bouquet garni (see Chef's tip)
4 cloves garlic, chopped
2 cups chicken stock or water
32–40 large pasta shells (conchiglioni)
1 lb. ricotta cheese
1/4 cup freshly grated Parmesan
2 eggs
1 tablespoon chopped fresh parsley
1 tablespoon chopped fresh basil
1/4 teaspoon grated nutmeg
8 oz. fresh mozzarella or bocconcini, sliced or shredded

1 Preheat the oven to 350°F. To make the tomato sauce, melt the butter over medium heat in a large flameproof casserole or Dutch oven. Add the bacon and cook until golden brown. Add the onion and carrot and cook for 3 minutes. Add the tomato paste, stir well and cook for another 2 minutes. Sprinkle with the flour and place in the oven for 5 minutes. Remove and stir well until the flour disappears, then add the tomatoes, bouquet garni and garlic. Cook on the stove for 5 minutes, stirring well, then add the stock or water, bring to a boil, stirring, and cook for 2 minutes. Cover and bake for 1 hour.

2 Bring a large saucepan of salted water to a boil. Add a splash of oil to stop the pasta from sticking and cook the shells according to the manufacturer's instructions. Drain and drizzle with a little olive oil. Arrange on a damp towel.

3 Lightly oil a large baking dish. In a bowl, mix together the ricotta, Parmesan, eggs, herbs and nutmeg and season with salt and pepper. Spoon the mixture into a pastry bag with a plain nozzle, fill each shell and arrange in a single layer in the prepared dish.

4 Strain the tomato sauce through a strainer, pressing well in order to extract as much liquid as possible. Discard the solids. Bring the sauce back to a boil and skim if necessary. Simmer for 20 minutes, or until the sauce thickens. Pour over the stuffed shells. Sprinkle the mozzarella over the sauce and bake for 30–40 minutes, or until the cheese is melted and browned.

Chef's tip To make the bouquet garni, wrap the green part of a leek loosely around a bay leaf, a sprig of thyme, some celery leaves and a few stalks of parsley. Tie the herbs with string, leaving a long tail to the string for easy removal.

Penne piselli

It is piselli, *the Italian word for peas, that lends its name to this dish—full of the flavors of bacon and peas in a rich creamy sauce.*

Preparation time **15 minutes**
Total cooking time **40 minutes**
Serves 4

10 oz. slab bacon, cut into $^1/_2$**-inch cubes**
3 tablespoons oil
1 large onion, finely chopped
2 cups heavy cream
1 cup shelled peas, fresh or frozen
1 lb. dried penne
3 tablespoons freshly grated Parmesan
fresh Parmesan shavings, to serve

1 In a saucepan, cover the bacon with cold water. Bring to a boil, drain and refresh in cold water, then drain again and pat dry. Heat the oil in a nonstick skillet over medium heat and cook the bacon for 3–4 minutes, or until lightly colored. Add the onion and cook for about 3–5 minutes, or until soft. Drain to remove any excess oil, place the cooked bacon and onion in a saucepan and add the cream. Bring to a boil, reduce the heat and simmer for 10 minutes.

2 Cook the peas in boiling salted water for about 3–5 minutes, or until tender. Drain and refresh in iced water. Drain again, add to the hot cream mixture and simmer for 3–5 minutes.

3 Bring a large saucepan of salted water to a boil. Add a splash of oil to stop the pasta from sticking and cook the penne according to the manufacturer's instructions. Drain well.

4 Toss the sauce and grated Parmesan through the pasta and serve topped with Parmesan shavings.

Roman gnocchi

The extremely popular Italian gnocchi can be made from potato, winter squash or, as in this case, semolina. Often served as a starter, gnocchi are also perfect for lunch, acccompanied by a crisp green salad.

Preparation time **35 minutes + 30 minutes cooling**
Total cooking time **2 hours 20 minutes**
Serves 4 as a starter

3 tablespoons unsalted butter
2 oz. bacon, diced
I small onion, chopped
I small carrot, chopped
3 tablespoons tomato paste
I tablespoon all-purpose flour
I lb. tomatoes, peeled, seeded and chopped
bouquet garni
4 cloves garlic, chopped
2 cups chicken stock or water

GNOCCHI
2 cups milk
¹/4 cup unsalted butter
I¹/4 cups semolina flour or fine semolina
¹/4 cup all-purpose flour
3 tablespoons heavy cream
I egg
2 egg yolks
¹/3 cup freshly grated Parmesan
¹/3 cup unsalted butter, melted

1 Preheat the oven to 350°F. Melt the butter in a small flameproof casserole and cook the bacon until golden brown. Add the onion and carrot and cook for 3 minutes. Stir in the tomato paste and cook for 2 minutes. Sprinkle with the flour, place in the oven for 5 minutes, then stir until the flour disappears. Add the tomatoes, bouquet garni and garlic, return to the stove top and cook for 5 minutes, stirring. Stir in the stock and boil for 2 minutes. Cover and bake for 1 hour. Strain into a clean saucepan and discard the solids. Bring the sauce back to a boil on the stove top and skim if necessary. Lower the heat and simmer for 20 minutes, or until thick enough to coat the back of a spoon. Season with salt and pepper, set aside and keep warm.

2 To make the gnocchi, bring the milk and butter to a boil in a large saucepan. Add the flours and stir over low heat until absorbed, then stir for 5 minutes longer, or until the mixture rolls off the side of the pan. Remove from the heat, add the cream, egg, egg yolks and half the Parmesan and stir until smooth. Season to taste and spread ¹/2 inch thick on a baking sheet lined with waxed paper. Cool for 30 minutes, then cut into rounds with a wet 1¹/2-inch cutter. Put in a baking dish, drizzle with the melted butter and sprinkle with the remaining Parmesan. Bake for 20 minutes, or until golden, and serve with the tomato sauce.

Saffron pasta with spinach and ricotta

The bright yellow saffron pasta needed for this particular recipe is as simple to make as plain fresh pasta. Teamed with a delicious spinach and ricotta sauce, this dish is perfect for vegetarians.

Preparation time **50 minutes + 15 minutes soaking**
Total cooking time **10 minutes**
Serves 4

PASTA
pinch of saffron threads
2¹/2 cups all-purpose flour
1 teaspoon salt
2 teaspoons olive oil
3 eggs, lightly beaten

¹/2 cup whipping cream
¹/3 cup ricotta or cream cheese
¹/4 cup unsalted butter
2 cloves garlic, finely chopped
1 ¹/2 cups frozen spinach, thawed, drained and
finely chopped
pinch of freshly grated nutmeg
freshly grated Parmesan, to serve

1 To make the pasta, soak the saffron in 1 tablespoon hot water for 15 minutes, then follow the method in the Chef's techniques on page 62, adding the saffron threads and their liquid along with the eggs. Divide the dough into four pieces before passing through the pasta machine. When the pasta has passed through the thinnest setting, pass the sheets through the ¹/4-inch cutters to make tagliatelle (see Chef's techniques, page 63).

2 Blend the cream and ricotta or cream cheese together in a blender or food processor. Melt the butter with the garlic over medium heat in a skillet. When the butter stops sizzling, add the chopped spinach and sauté for 2–3 minutes. Remove from the heat, cool slightly, then stir in the ricotta and cream mixture, seasoning well with some salt, freshly ground black pepper and the grated nutmeg.

3 Bring a large saucepan of salted water to a boil. Add a splash of oil to stop the pasta from sticking and cook the tagliatelle for 2–3 minutes, or until *al dente*. Drain the pasta well.

4 Return the pasta to the pan, toss with the spinach and ricotta sauce and heat through for a moment. Serve on four warm plates with a bowl of the grated Parmesan on the side.

Tomato pasta with fennel and bell peppers

A celebration of vibrant Mediterranean flavors with a refreshing lemon lift. This sauce could also be served with plain fresh tagliatelle or dried pasta if short of time.

Preparation time **1 hour**
Total cooking time **1 hour 10 minutes**
Serves 4

PASTA
2¹/₂ cups all-purpose flour
1 teaspoon salt
2 tablespoons olive oil
3 eggs, lightly beaten
4 teaspoons sun-dried tomato paste or tomato paste

1 medium fennel bulb
olive oil, for cooking
1 red bell pepper
2 cloves garlic, crushed
1 x 16 oz. can chopped plum tomatoes
grated rind of ¹/₂ lemon
sprig of fresh thyme

1 To make the pasta, see the Chef's techniques on page 62, and add the tomato paste with the eggs.
2 Divide the dough into four pieces before passing through the pasta machine. When the pasta has passed through the thinnest setting, pass the sheets through the ¹/₄-inch cutters to make tagliatelle (see Chef's techniques, page 63). Preheat the oven to 400°F. Trim the stalks from the top of the fennel. Cut the bulb in half lengthwise, then into ³/₄-inch wide lengths. Place in a saucepan of boiling water and simmer for 8–10 minutes, or until just tender when pierced. Drain, place to one end of a greased baking sheet and drizzle with a tablespoon of olive oil.
3 Cut the red pepper in half and remove the seeds. Brush with oil and place, skin-side-up, on the other end of the baking sheet. Bake for 15 minutes, or until the fennel is golden, turning once during cooking. Remove the fennel. Increase the oven temperature to 425°F and bake the pepper for another 10 minutes, or until the skin is blackened. Place in a plastic bag to cool.
4 Heat 2 tablespoons olive oil in a saucepan, add the garlic and cook gently until light brown. Add the tomatoes, lemon rind and thyme and simmer for 20–25 minutes, or until thick and pulpy. Remove the thyme and season.
5 Cut the fennel into small pieces. Peel off and discard the skin from the pepper and cut into thin strips. Add them both to the tomato mixture and season.
6 Bring a large saucepan of salted water to a boil. Add a splash of oil to stop the pasta from sticking and cook the tagliatelle for 2–3 minutes, or until *al dente*. Drain the pasta well, toss with the sauce and serve.

Vegetable lasagna

Try this deliciously different lasagna with its crunchy vegetables and cheese sauce with a hint of nutmeg.
Making your own pasta is both enjoyable and satisfying.

*Preparation time **1 hour + 30 minutes resting***
*Total cooking time **1 hour 30 minutes***
Serves 6

PASTA
2¹/₂ cups all-purpose flour
1 teaspoon salt
2 tablespoons olive oil
3 eggs, lightly beaten

CHEESE SAUCE
2 tablespoons unsalted butter
¹/₄ cup all-purpose flour
2 cups milk
¹/₄ teaspoon ground nutmeg
¹/₃ cup whipping cream
³/₄ cup shredded Gruyère cheese

2 tablespoons unsalted butter
1 small onion, sliced
4 ripe tomatoes, peeled, seeded
  and chopped
1 sprig of fresh thyme
1 bay leaf
1¹/₃ cups diced carrots
4 cups small broccoli florets
¹/₂ cauliflower, cut into florets
²/₃ cup shredded Gruyère cheese

1 To make the pasta, follow the method in the Chef's techniques on page 62, dividing the dough into four pieces before passing through the pasta machine to a thickness of ¹/₁₆–¹/₈ inch. Cut the sheets with a sharp knife into noodles about 6 x 3 inches long.

2 Bring a large saucepan of salted water to a boil. Add a splash of oil to stop the pasta from sticking and cook the lasagne in batches for 2–3 minutes, or until *al dente*. Transfer to a bowl of cold water, drain and put between layers of clean towel.

3 To make the cheese sauce, melt the butter in a saucepan, stir in the flour with a wooden spoon and cook gently for 3 minutes, stirring constantly. Remove from the heat and gradually stir in the cold milk. Blend thoroughly, season with salt and pepper and add the nutmeg. Return to the heat and bring slowly to a boil, stirring constantly. Lower the heat and cook, stirring, for about 7 minutes, or until thickened. Stir in the cream and cheese. Remove from the heat and cover the surface with buttered waxed paper.

4 Heat the butter in a skillet and cook the onion slowly without browning. Add the tomatoes, thyme and bay leaf. Simmer for 15 minutes, or until pulpy. Discard the bay leaf and thyme and season with salt and pepper.

5 Bring a large saucepan of salted water to a boil. Add the carrots, reduce the heat and simmer for 4 minutes. Add the broccoli and cauliflower and simmer for 3 minutes. Drain the vegetables and refresh with cold water to stop the cooking process. Drain well and set aside.

6 Preheat the oven to 375°F. Mix the cheese and tomato sauces and simmer for 15 minutes. Add the vegetables to the sauce. Season. Butter a 2–2¹/₂-quart baking dish and alternate layers of pasta and vegetable mixture, finishing with pasta. Sprinkle the cheese over the top and bake for 35 minutes.

Carrot pasta with bell peppers, snow peas and Parmesan

The combination of carrot pasta tossed in a light carrot sauce with vegetables, black olives, basil and a sprinkling of Parmesan makes this an unusual yet excellent pasta dish.

Preparation time **1 hour**
Total cooking time **30 minutes**
Serves 4

CARROT PASTA
3 medium carrots, sliced
2 cups all-purpose flour
1 teaspoon salt
1 tablespoon olive oil
4 egg yolks, lightly beaten

1 large red bell pepper
24 snow peas
1/3 cup unsalted butter, chilled and cut in cubes
large pinch of ground nutmeg
1/4 cup shredded fresh basil leaves
1/4 cup small black olives, pitted and halved
1 cup freshly grated Parmesan

1 Place the carrots and 3/4 cup water in a blender and process until smooth and thick. Transfer a quarter of this juice to a small saucepan, reserving the rest, and boil over medium heat for 10 minutes, or until it reduces to about 1/3 cup of thick purée. Remove and cool.

2 To make the pasta, follow the method in the Chef's techniques on page 62, and add the carrot purée with the eggs. Divide the dough into four pieces before passing through the pasta machine. When the pasta has passed through the thinnest setting, pass the sheets through the 1/4-inch cutters to make tagliatelle (see Chef's techniques, page 63).

3 Preheat the broiler to a high setting, lightly oil the red pepper and place under the broiler, turning carefully, until it is blackened and blistered. Place the pepper in a plastic bag to cool. Peel, halve, seed, and cut the pepper into 1/4-inch strips, then set aside and keep warm.

4 Bring a large saucepan of salted water to a boil. Add a splash of oil to stop the pasta from sticking and cook the tagliatelle for 2–3 minutes, or until *al dente*. Drain, run under cold water, then drain once more. Heat 1/4 inch of oil in the pan and quickly toss in the pasta. Remove, cover and keep to one side.

5 Plunge the snow peas into a saucepan of boiling salted water, then drain and keep warm. In a pan, bring the reserved carrot juice to a boil. Lower the heat, whisk in the butter to form a thickened sauce and season with nutmeg, salt and pepper. Add the sauce to the pasta and reheat. Then add the snow peas, pepper, basil, olives and half the Parmesan. Serve sprinkled with the remaining Parmesan.

Spaghetti alla diavola

Diavola, *meaning devil in Italian, refers to any dish that has been enlivened with hot pepper and garlic. Sometimes simple is better, so here is a recipe that is simply spicy, garlicky and good.*

Preparation time **15 minutes**
Total cooking time **15 minutes**
Serves 4

I lb. dried spaghetti
I cup olive oil
2 heads of garlic, peeled and sliced
1/2–I teaspoon dried hot red pepper flakes, or to taste
chopped fresh flat-leaf parsley, to serve
freshly grated Parmesan, to serve

1 Bring a large saucepan of salted water to a boil. Add a splash of oil to stop the pasta from sticking and cook the pasta according to the manufacturer's instructions.
2 While the pasta is cooking, heat the oil in a deep skillet over medium heat. Add the garlic and hot pepper flakes and cook for 10–15 minutes, or until the garlic starts to brown slightly. Drain the pasta thoroughly and toss with the hot sauce. Season to taste.
3 Sprinkle with chopped parsley and serve with the freshly grated Parmesan.

Chef's tip Use the dried red pepper flakes with discretion—some are much hotter than others.

Linguine with Gorgonzola sauce

If Gorgonzola is unavailable, any mild blue cheese could be used in its place.

Preparation time **10 minutes**
Total cooking time **15 minutes**
Serves 4–6

I lb. dried linguine
1 1/4 cups heavy cream, at room temperature
10 oz. Gorgonzola or similar blue cheese, cut
   into cubes

1 Bring a large saucepan of salted water to a boil. Add a splash of oil to stop the pasta from sticking and cook the pasta according to the manufacturer's instructions.
2 Meanwhile, in a heavy-bottomed saucepan, bring the cream to a boil. Remove from the heat and whisk in the cheese until smooth. Strain through a fine sieve.
3 Drain the linguine and toss it with the hot sauce. Serve immediately.

Spaghetti alla diavola (top) and Linguine with Gorgonzola sauce

Ziti amatriciana

*The ziti used in this recipe are very long thin tubes.
If unavailable, use macaroni or penne.*

Preparation time **15 minutes**
Total cooking time **50 minutes**
Serves 4–6

3 tablespoons olive oil
12 oz. pancetta or bacon, cut into 1/4-inch
  thick pieces
1 onion, thinly sliced
2–3 fresh chiles, thinly sliced or 1/2 teaspoon dried hot
  red pepper flakes
2 x 16 oz. cans chopped plum tomatoes
  or 31/2 lb. fresh tomatoes, peeled and chopped
1 lb. dried ziti
freshly grated Parmesan, to serve

1 In a heavy-bottomed saucepan, heat half the oil and
slowly brown the pancetta or bacon for 5 minutes, then
drain and set aside on paper towels. Add the onion and
lightly brown for about 3 minutes, then add the chiles
or hot pepper flakes and cook for 2 minutes. Add the
pancetta or bacon and the tomatoes, cover and cook
over medium heat for about 20 minutes, then cook
uncovered for another 10–15 minutes, or until thick.
2 Bring a large saucepan of salted water to a boil. Add
a splash of oil to stop the pasta from sticking and cook
the ziti according to the manufacturer's instructions.
3 Drain the pasta and serve with the sauce and freshly
grated Parmesan.

Chef's tip The degree of spiciness depends on the
chiles available. Remember that most of the heat is in
the seeds and membranes. Be careful when handling the
chiles and keep your fingers away from your face.

Ravioli in rosemary garlic cream

It is not until you cut the ravioli that you discover the colorful mixture of vegetables hidden within the thin pasta casing. The delicious garlic sauce perfectly complements the vegetable filling in flavor and texture.

*Preparation time **1 hour 10 minutes***
*Total cooking time **1 hour 30 minutes***
Serves 4

PASTA
1²/₃ cups all-purpose flour
pinch of salt
4 teaspoons olive oil
2 eggs, lightly beaten

VEGETABLE FILLING
2 tablespoons unsalted butter
1 shallot, finely chopped
12 mushroom caps, finely chopped
juice of ¹/₄ lemon
¹/₂ carrot, finely diced
1 small zucchini, with the spongy center scraped out,
   finely diced
3 tablespoons heavy cream

SAUCE
2 cups chicken stock
8 cloves garlic, peeled
sprig of fresh rosemary, cut into
   1¹/₄-inch pieces
2 cups heavy cream

1 egg, lightly beaten
freshly grated Parmesan, to serve

1 To make the pasta, follow the method in the Chef's techniques on page 62, dividing the dough into two pieces before passing through the pasta machine. Pass the pieces through the thinnest setting on the machine to make two long strips.

2 To make the vegetable filling, melt the butter over low heat in a medium skillet and cook the shallot for 3 minutes. Mix the mushrooms with the lemon juice and add to the pan with a good pinch of salt. Cook for about 10 minutes, stirring constantly, until the mushrooms are dry. Set aside.

3 Cook the carrot in boiling salted water for 2 minutes, or until tender. Refresh in cold water, drain and pat dry on paper towels. Cook the zucchini for 1 minute in boiling salted water, refresh, drain and pat dry. Add the cooked vegetables to the mushroom mixture. Put the pan back on the heat and add the cream. Cook for about 5–7 minutes over low heat, or until almost dry. Season and set aside to cool completely.

4 To make the sauce, cook the chicken stock with the garlic over high heat for about 20 minutes, or until it is syrupy and just a few tablespoons are left. Remove from the heat, add the rosemary and allow to infuse until cooled. Remove the rosemary and transfer the sauce to a blender. Blend until smooth. Strain into a small saucepan and add the cream. Bring to a simmer and cook for 35–40 minutes, or until the sauce is thick enough to coat the back of a spoon. Season to taste and keep warm.

5 Take one strip of dough and mark with a 1¹/₂-inch round biscuit cutter, leaving a small space between each mark. Place a small amount of the filling in the center of each of the marks. Lightly brush around each ball of filling with a little of the egg. Place the other pasta sheet on top and press firmly around each mound to expel any air and to seal. Use the biscuit cutter to cut the dough. Place the ravioli in a single layer between sheets of waxed paper and refrigerate until ready to use (see Chef's techniques, page 63).

6 Bring a large saucepan of salted water to a boil. Add a splash of oil to stop the pasta from sticking and cook the ravioli for 2–3 minutes, or until *al dente*. Drain and serve with the sauce and Parmesan.

Parisian gnocchi

Gnocchi is Italian for dumpling and they are usually made with potatoes, flour or semolina. However, in this recipe they are shaped from a kind of choux pastry, which makes them beautifully light.

Preparation time **30 minutes**
Total cooking time **40 minutes**
Serves 4 as a first course

GNOCCHI DOUGH
pinch of ground nutmeg
2 tablespoons unsalted butter
1/2 cup all-purpose flour
2 eggs, beaten
2 tablespoons shredded Gruyère cheese

BECHAMEL SAUCE
1 tablespoon unsalted butter
3 tablespoons all-purpose flour
1 cup milk
2/3 cup chopped ham
1/3 cup shredded Gruyère cheese

1 To make the gnocchi dough, place the nutmeg, butter, some salt and pepper and 1/2 cup water in a saucepan and bring to a boil. Sift the flour and mix in with a wooden spoon until a ball starts to form and pulls away from the sides of the pan. Place in a bowl, cool, then add the eggs slowly, beating well after each addition until smooth. Stir in the cheese and set the dough aside.

2 To make the béchamel sauce, melt the butter in a saucepan over low heat and add the flour. Stir until a smooth paste forms, then cook for 3 minutes. Remove from the heat and cool. In another saucepan, bring the milk to a boil, then whisk into the cooled mixture. Bring to a boil slowly, stirring constantly to stop lumps from forming. Remove from the heat, add the ham and cheese and season with salt and black pepper.

3 Preheat the oven to 325°F. Bring a saucepan of salted water to a boil and prepare a large bowl of cold water. Place the dough in a pastry bag fitted with a medium-size plain round nozzle and pipe gnocchi into the boiling water, cutting into 1-inch lengths with a knife. Once the gnocchi rise to the surface, cook for just 30 seconds, then remove. Place in the cold water, then drain on a clean cloth.

4 Butter a baking dish and sprinkle with salt and freshly ground black pepper. Pour in about a quarter of the béchamel sauce. Arrange the gnocchi in layers, coating each layer with some of the sauce, then finishing with a layer of sauce. Bake for 10 minutes, then increase the temperature to 400°F and bake the gnocchi until the top is nicely golden.

Herb tagliatelle with mushrooms and olive oil

This recipe calls for herb tagliatelle. However, if time is short, it could be made with fresh, plain or spinach tagliatelle bought from a specialty market or good supermarket. Serve with a crisp green salad.

Preparation time 30 minutes
Total cooking time 15 minutes
Serves 6

HERB TAGLIATELLE
2¹/2 cups all-purpose flour
1 teaspoon salt
2 tablespoons olive oil
3 eggs, lightly beaten
3 tablespoons finely chopped fresh herbs, such as tarragon, parsley or basil leaves

2 tablespoons unsalted butter
3 shallots, chopped
12 oz. mushrooms (button or a mixture of button and wild mushrooms), sliced
1 tablespoon sherry or Marsala
¹/3 cup olive oil
5 large tomatoes, peeled, seeded and chopped
¹/2 cup chopped mixed fresh herbs
2 tablespoons shredded basil leaves or chopped oregano, to garnish
Parmesan shavings, to serve

1 To make the pasta, follow the method in the Chef's techniques on page 62, and add the chopped herbs with the eggs. Divide the dough into four pieces before passing through the pasta machine. When the pasta has passed through the thinnest setting, pass the sheets through the ¹/4-inch cutters to make tagliatelle (see Chef's techniques, page 63).

2 Heat the butter in a skillet over medium heat, add the shallots and cook until soft but not colored. Turn up the heat, toss in the mushrooms and fry until they start to color. Continue to cook for 2–3 minutes. Add the sherry or Marsala and cook for 30 seconds. Season and set aside.

3 Bring a large saucepan of salted water to a boil. Add a splash of oil to stop the pasta from sticking and cook the tagliatelle for 2–3 minutes, or until *al dente*. Drain well and set aside.

4 Heat the olive oil in a large saucepan over medium heat and add the mushroom mixture, the herb tagliatelle, tomatoes and mixed herbs. Heat the mixture through and season generously with salt and freshly ground black pepper. Garnish with the shredded basil or chopped oregano and serve immediately with the Parmesan shavings.

Seafood lasagna

Layers of homemade pasta, fresh fish and seafood, creamy white sauce and mozzarella make this a truly memorable dish. Of course, store-bought lasagna noodles could be used if you're short of time.

Preparation time **1 hour 35 minutes**
Total cooking time **1 hour 20 minutes**
Serves 12

PASTA
2¹/₂ *cups all-purpose flour*
1 teaspoon salt
2 tablespoons olive oil
3 eggs, lightly beaten

4 shallots, finely chopped
1¹/₂ cups dry white wine
2 sprigs of fresh thyme
1 bay leaf
2 lb. fresh mussels, scrubbed clean
1¹/₄ lb. fresh or frozen thawed scallops,
  patted dry
1¹/₄ lb. boneless cod, cubed
1¹/₄ lb. cooked peeled shrimp, patted dry
1 lb. mozzarella, thinly sliced

SAUCE
¹/₄ *cup unsalted butter*
³/₄ *cup all-purpose flour*
2¹/₃ *cups whipping cream*
1 lb. ricotta cheese

1 To make the pasta, follow the method in the Chef's techniques on page 62, dividing the dough into four pieces before passing through the pasta machine to a thickness of ¹/₁₆ inch. Cut the sheets with a sharp knife into small rectangles about 5 x 4 inches long.
2 Bring a large saucepan of salted water to a boil. Add a splash of oil to stop the pasta from sticking and cook the lasagna in batches for 1–2 minutes, or until *al dente*.

Transfer to a bowl of cold water, drain and put between layers of clean towels.
3 Place the shallots, wine, thyme and bay leaf in a large saucepan and bring to a boil. Add the mussels and simmer, covered, for 5 minutes, or until the mussels have opened. Remove with a slotted spoon, discard the shells and any unopened mussels. Drain on paper towels. Add the scallops and poach for 3 minutes, then drain on paper towels. Strain the cooking liquid through a strainer lined with damp cheesecloth. Rinse the pan, return the liquid to the pan, heat until simmering and add the cod. Poach for 3–5 minutes, then drain on paper towels. Measure out 2 cups of the cooking liquid, return it to the pan and simmer for 10 minutes, skimming any foam from the surface. Set aside to cool.
4 To make the sauce, melt the butter in a small saucepan, add the flour and cook for 2 minutes without coloring. Remove from the heat and gradually add the cooking liquid, stirring constantly. Return to the heat and bring to a boil, stirring, then simmer for 3 minutes. Add the cream and simmer for 5 minutes. Season well.
5 Preheat the oven to 350°F. Combine all the seafood and ¹/₄ cup of the sauce in a bowl. Combine the ricotta and 1 cup of the sauce in another bowl.
6 Butter a 9 x 13-inch baking dish. Coat the bottom with a little of the sauce. Cover with a layer of pasta, then with a third of the seafood mixture. With a spoon or spatula, roughly spread a third of the ricotta mixture over the seafood as evenly as possible, then cover with a layer of the mozzarella and finally spoon on about ¹/₂ cup of the sauce. Sprinkle with salt and pepper. Repeat twice more, reserving some of the sauce for the top. Cover with a final layer of pasta, then the remaining sauce. Arrange the remaining mozzarella to cover the top and bake for 25 minutes, or until bubbly and lightly colored. Allow to cool for about 5 minutes before cutting.

Spaghetti puttanesca

A piquant combination of garlic, tomatoes, capers, olives and anchovies make up this popular Italian sauce.

*Preparation time **35 minutes***
*Total cooking time **50 minutes***
Serves 4

1/4 cup olive oil
4 cloves garlic, chopped
13/4 lb. tomatoes, peeled, seeded and chopped
1/4–1/2 teaspoon dried hot red pepper flakes
3 tablespoons capers, drained
1 cup pitted black olives
3/4 cup chicken stock or water
1–11/4 oz. can of anchovy fillets, drained and
    coarsely chopped
3 tablespoons chopped fresh basil
3 tablespoons chopped fresh parsley
1 lb. dried spaghetti

1 In a medium saucepan, heat the oil over low heat and cook the garlic for 1 minute, without browning. Add the tomatoes, red pepper flakes, capers, olives and stock or water. Bring to a boil and cook over medium heat, covered, for 20 minutes. Remove the cover and simmer for another 25 minutes. Once the sauce is cooked, mix in the anchovies, basil and parsley.
2 Bring a large saucepan of salted water to a boil. Add a splash of oil to stop the pasta from sticking and cook the pasta according to the manufacturer's instructions. Drain and toss with the hot sauce and serve.

Sicilian-style pasta

Tuna and sardines are the most common fish in Sicily, hence the name of this tuna pasta.

*Preparation time **30 minutes***
*Total cooking time **50 minutes***
Serves 6

1/2 cup olive oil
2 small onions, finely chopped
11/2 lb. tomatoes, peeled, seeded and chopped
3 cloves garlic, crushed
bouquet garni (See Chef's tip)
1/2 cup pitted and chopped black olives
2 cups sliced button mushrooms
1 lb. fresh tuna, cut into 1/2-inch cubes
1 lb. dried pappardelle (wide noodles)
3 tablespoons chopped fresh parsley
3 tablespoons freshly grated Parmesan

1 Heat a third of the olive oil in a heavy-bottomed saucepan and cook the onions until translucent. Add the tomatoes, garlic and bouquet garni and cook gently for 30–35 minutes. At the end of the cooking, mix in the black olives. In a skillet, sauté the mushrooms in a third of the olive oil. Season and transfer to a strainer to drain.
2 In the skillet, heat the remaining oil over high heat. Lightly season the tuna, then sauté in the hot oil.
3 Bring a large saucepan of salted water to a boil. Add a splash of oil to stop the pasta from sticking and cook the psta according to the manufacturer's instructions. Drain and place in a large bowl. Add the tomato sauce, tuna and mushrooms and toss well. Sprinkle with the parsley and Parmesan and serve immediately.

Chef's tip To make the bouquet garni, wrap the green part of a leek around a bay leaf, a sprig of thyme, some celery leaves and a few stalks of parsley. Tie with string, leaving a long tail to the string for easy removal.

Chef's techniques

◆

Making pasta

See the list of ingredients in each pasta recipe to find out the quantity of flour, salt, olive oil and eggs needed to make the pasta dough for each dish. Fresh pasta should be used on the same day it is made.

Place the flour, salt, olive oil and eggs or egg yolks in a food processor and mix in short bursts until the mixture forms large crumbs.

Gently press the mixture between your finger and thumb to check if it will come together smoothly. If not, continue to process for a few bursts.

Turn out onto a lightly floured surface and knead for 2 minutes into a smooth dough. Wrap in plastic wrap and refrigerate for 20 minutes. Secure a pasta machine to the edge of a table.

Divide the dough into as many pieces as specified in the recipe. Keep covered and work with one piece at a time. Flatten into a rectangle and roll through the lightly floured pasta machine on the thickest setting.

Fold the sheet into thirds and pass through the machine again at the thickest setting. Repeat this rolling and folding ten times, lightly flouring the pasta dough and machine to prevent sticking.

Without folding, continue to pass the dough through progressively thinner settings, until it has passed through the finest setting. Repeat with the remaining pieces of dough.

Making pasta by hand

This is the traditional method for making pasta without a food processor.

Sift the flour and salt onto a work surface. Make a large well in the center with your hand and add the eggs or egg yolks, and olive oil.

Using your fingertips, gradually incorporate the flour into the wet ingredients.

With a pastry scraper or by hand, keep bringing the flour into the center, making a dough. Knead for 10 minutes, or until smooth and elastic. Divide into pieces as specified in the recipe. Cover with plastic wrap.

Rolling out pasta by hand

Use a large, lightly floured work surface so the dough can be rolled out to a very large sheet.

Roll out the dough as thinly as possible, fold in half and roll again, bringing the furthest end over the rolling pin and gently stretching it. Roll and fold the dough ten times. Roll out to the thickness required.

Making ravioli

The uncooked ravioli may be refrigerated or frozen in single layers between sheets of waxed paper.

Lightly brush a little water or egg around each mound of filling.

Place the second sheet of pasta on top and press firmly around each mound to expel any air and to seal. Using a rolling cutter or biscuit cutter, cut out each ravioli.

Alternatively, use the ravioli cutter on a pasta machine. Place two pasta sheets into the floured machine and two mounds of filling in the grooves. Turn the handle of the machine to cut.

Making tagliatelle

The tagliatelle may be dried on a floured towel hanging over the back of a chair for 1–2 hours.

Pass the sheet of pasta through a floured pasta machine fitted with the tagliatelle attachment. Or roll up the sheet of pasta and cut into ribbons with a knife. Cook immediately or allow to dry in a single layer.

First published in the United States in 1998 by Periplus Editions (HK) Ltd., with editorial offices at
153 Milk Street, Boston, Massachusetts 02109.

Murdoch Books and Le Cordon Bleu thank the 32 masterchefs of all the Le Cordon Bleu Schools, whose knowledge and
expertise have made this book possible, especially: Chef Cliche (MOF), Chef Terrien, Chef Boucheret, Chef Duchêne (MOF),
Chef Guillut, Chef Steneck, Paris; Chef Males, Chef Walsh, Chef Hardy, London; Chef Chantefort, Chef Bertin, Chef Jambert,
Chef Honda, Tokyo; Chef Salembien, Chef Boutin, Chef Harris, Sydney; Chef Lawes, Adelaide; Chef Guiet, Chef Denis, Ottawa.
Of the many students who helped the Chefs test each recipe, a special mention to graduates David Welch and Allen Wertheim.
A very special acknowledgment to Directors Susan Eckstein, Great Britain, and Kathy Shaw, Paris, who have been responsible for
the coordination of the Le Cordon Bleu team throughout this series.

The Publisher and Le Cordon Bleu also wish to thank Carole Sweetnam for her help with this series.

First published in Australia in 1998 by Murdoch Books®

Managing Editor: Kay Halsey
Series Concept, Design and Art Direction: Juliet Cohen
Food Director: Jody Vassallo
Food Editors: Dimitra Stais, Tracy Rutherford
US Editor: Linda Venturoni Wilson
Designer: Michèle Lichtenberger
Photographer: Joe Filshie
Food Stylist: Carolyn Fienberg
Food Preparation: Jo Forrest
Chef's Techniques Photographer: Reg Morrison
Home Economists: Joanna Beaumont, Michelle Lawton, Kerrie Mullins, Justine Poole, Kerrie Ray, Margot Smithyman

©Design and photography Murdoch Books® 1998
©Text Le Cordon Bleu 1998. The moral right of Le Cordon Bleu has been asserted with respect to this publication.

All rights reserved. No part of this publication may be reproduced or utilized in any form or by any means,
electronic or mechanical, including photocopying, recording, or by any information storage and retrieval system,
without prior written permission from Periplus Editions

Library of Congress catalog card number: 98-85719
ISBN 962-593-446-4

Front cover: Pumpkin ravioli with basil butter

Distributed in the United States by
Charles E. Tuttle Co., Inc.
RR1 Box 231-5
North Clarendon, VT 05759
Tel: (802) 773-8930
Fax: (802) 773-6993

Printed in Singapore

05 04 03 02 01 00 99 98 10 9 8 7 6 5 4 3 2 1

Important: Some of the recipes in this book may include raw eggs, which can cause salmonella poisoning.
Those who might be at risk from this (the elderly, pregnant women, young children and those suffering
from immune deficiency diseases) should check with their physicians before eating raw eggs.